For photographic acknowledgments and copyright
details, see pages 86-91 and page 93.

Cover and interior design by David Fordham
Set by MATS, Southend-on-Sea, Essex

First published in Great Britain in 1998 by
Frances Lincoln Limited, 4 Torriano Mews,
Torriano Avenue, London NW5 2RZ.
This edition first published in 2000 by Contemporary Books
A division of NTC/Contemporary Publishing Group, Inc. 4255
West Touhy Avenue, Lincolnwood (Chicago),
Illinois 60712-1975, USA.

Printed in Hong Kong
International Standard Book Number: 0-8092-2426-7

Library of Congress Cataloging-in-Publication Data is available
from the United States Library of Congress.

LOVE IS ENOUGH

❧ POEMS AND PAINTINGS CELEBRATING LOVE ❧

CB
CONTEMPORARY BOOKS

∼ PREFACE ∼

The lovers' tradition of communicating through poetry is as old as the world itself. Poetry has the power to vanquish the unconquerable heart and to state profound truths about the nature of love, truths as relevant today as in the past. In just a few words a poem can express what books of prose often cannot.

In this special collection, poets such as Keats, Shelley, Wordsworth, and Tennyson reveal the many facets of love. Each poem is a love letter meant to be shared between lover and beloved. The poets convey many of the emotions bound to love, including joy and despair.

Some of these poems are classics; others are less well known but no less evocative. Many of the poems are tributes to spiritual and physical beauty, some use images of nature and religion in order to commemorate idealized love, but all are expressions of the poets' visions of love, from the sentimental to the sublime.

There are many ways in which love poems touch our hearts and souls, but perhaps the most outstanding is the poet's ability to put into words something as elusive as love. "Poetry should be great and unobtrusive," said John Keats, "a thing which enters into one's soul, and does not startle or amaze with itself, but with its subject." The poems in this collection perfectly capture that sentiment.

"Its passions will rock thee
As the storms rock the ravens on high..."

—"The Flight of Love"
by Percy Bysshe Shelley

~ Love-Lily ~

DANTE GABRIEL ROSSETTI

Between the hands, between the brows,
    Between the lips of Love-Lily,
A spirit is born whose birth endows
    My blood with fire to burn through me;
Who breathes upon my gazing eyes,
    Who laughs and murmurs in mine ear,
At whose least touch my colour flies,
    And whom my life grows faint to hear.

Within the voice, within the heart,
    Within the mind of Love-Lily,
A spirit is born who lifts apart
    His tremulous wings and looks at me;
Who on my mouth his finger lays,
    And shows, while whispering lutes confer,
That Eden of Love's watered ways
    Whose winds and spirits worship her.

Brows, hands, and lips, heart, mind, and voice,
    Kisses and words of Love-Lily,—
Oh! bid me with your joy rejoice
    Till riotous longing rest in me!
Ah! let not hope be still distraught,
    But find in her its gracious goal,
Whose speech Truth knows not from her thought
    Nor Love her body from her soul.

~ THE LOST LOVE ~

William Wordsworth

She dwelt among the untrodden ways
　　Beside the springs of Dove;
A maid whom there were none to praise,
　　And very few to love.

A violet by a mossy stone
　　Half-hidden from the eye!
—Fair as a star, when only one
　　Is shining in the sky.

She lived unknown, and few could know
　　When Lucy ceased to be;
But she is in her grave, and O!
　　The difference to me!

~ Music, ~
When Soft Voices Die

PERCY BYSSHE SHELLEY

Music, when soft voices die,
Vibrates in the memory;
Odours, when sweet violets sicken,
Live within the sense they quicken.

Rose leaves, when the rose is dead,
Are heaped for the belovèd's bed;
And so thy thoughts, when thou art gone,
Love itself shall slumber on.

~ℱor the Briar Rose~

William Morris

THE BRIARWOOD

The fateful slumber floats and flows
About the tangle of the rose;
But lo! the fated hand and heart
To rend the slumbrous curse apart!

THE COUNCIL ROOM

The threat of war, the hope of peace,
The Kingdom's peril and increase
Sleep on and bide the latter day,
When fate shall take her chain away.

THE GARDEN COURT

The maiden pleasance of the land
Knoweth no stir of voice or hand,
No cup the sleeping waters fill,
The restless shuttle lieth still.

THE ROSEBOWER

Here lies the hoarded love, the key
To all the treasure that shall be;
Come fated hand the gift to take,
And smite this sleeping world awake.

~ Another for ~ the Briar Rose

William Morris

ﾟ

O treacherous scent, O thorny sight,
O tangle of world's wrong and right,
What art thou 'gainst my armour's gleam
But dusky cobwebs of a dream?

Beat down, deep sunk from every gleam
Of hope, they lie and dully dream;
Men once, but men no more, that Love
Their waste defeated hearts should move.

Here sleeps the world that would not love!
Let it sleep on, but if He move
Their hearts in humble wise to wait
On his new-wakened fair estate.

O won at last is never late!
Thy silence was the voice of fate;
Thy still hands conquered in the strife;
Thine eyes were light; thy lips were life.

from

~ THE PRINCESS ~

ALFRED TENNYSON

Now sleeps the crimson petal, now the white;
Nor waves the cypress in the palace walk;
Nor winks the gold fin in the porphyry font:
The fire-fly wakens: waken thou with me.

Now droops the milkwhite peacock like a ghost,
And like a ghost she glimmers on to me.

Now lies the Earth all Danaë to the stars,
And all thy heart lies open unto me.

Now slides the silent meteor on, and leaves
A shining furrow, as thy thoughts in me.

Now folds the lily all her sweetness up,
And slips into the bosom of the lake:
So fold thyself, my dearest, thou, and slip
Into my bosom and be lost in me.

~ℒove is ℰnough~

WILLIAM MORRIS

ℒove is enough: though the World be a-waning,
　And the woods have no voice but the voice of complaining,
　Though the sky be too dark for dim eyes to discover
The gold-cups and daisies fair blooming thereunder,
Though the hills be held shadows, and the sea a dark wonder
　And this day draw a veil over all deeds passed over,
Yet their hands shall not tremble, their feet shall not falter;
The void shall not weary, the fear shall not alter
　These lips and these eyes of the loved and the lover.

~ *Body's Beauty* ~

DANTE GABRIEL ROSSETTI

Of Adam's first wife, Lilith, it is told
   (The witch he loved before the gift of Eve)
   That, ere the snake's, her sweet tongue could deceive,
And her enchanted hair was the first gold.
And still she sits, young while the earth is old,
   And, subtly of herself contemplative,
   Draws men to watch the bright web she can weave,
Till heart and body and life are in its hold.

The rose and poppy are her flowers; for where
   Is he not found, O Lilith, whom shed scent
And soft-shed kisses and soft sleep shall snare?
   Lo! As that youth's eyes burned at thine, so went
   Thy spell through him, and left his straight neck bent
And round his heart one strangling golden hair.

～ In an Artist's Studio ～

CHRISTINA ROSSETTI

One face looks out from all his canvases,
   One selfsame figure sits or walks or leans:
   We found her hidden just behind those screens,
That mirror gave back all her loveliness.
A queen in opal or in ruby dress,
   A nameless girl in freshest summer-greens,
   A saint, an angel—every canvas means
The same one meaning, neither more nor less.
He feeds upon her face by day and night,
   And she with true kind eyes looks back on him,
Fair as the moon and joyful as the light:
   Not wan with waiting, not with sorrow dim;
Not as she is, but was when hope shone bright;
   Not as she is, but as she fills his dream.

from

~ IDYLLS OF THE KING ~

ALFRED TENNYSON

*I*n Love, if Love be Love, if Love be ours,
Faith and unfaith can ne'er be equal powers:
Unfaith in aught is want of faith in all.

It is the little rift within the lute,
That by and by will make the music mute,
And ever widening slowly silence all.

The little rift within the lover's lute
Or little pitted speck in garnered fruit,
That rotting inward slowly moulders all.

It is not worth the keeping: let it go:
But shall it? answer, darling, answer, no.
And trust me not at all or all in all.

~ La Belle Dame sans Merci ~

John Keats

'O what can ail thee, knight-at-arms,
   Alone and palely loitering?
The sedge is withered from the lake,
      And no birds sing.

'O what can ail thee, knight-at-arms,
   So haggard and so woe-begone?
The squirrel's granary is full,
      And the harvest's done.

'I see a lily on thy brow,
   With anguish moist and fever dew;
And on thy cheeks a fading rose
      Fast withereth too.'

'I met a lady in the meads,
   Full beautiful—a faery's child,
Her hair was long, her foot was light,
      And her eyes were wild.

'I made a garland for her head,
   And bracelets too, and fragrant zone;
She looked at me as she did love,
      And made sweet moan.

'I set her on my pacing steed
   And nothing else saw all day long,
For sidelong would she bend, and sing
      A faery's song.

❦

'She found me roots of relish sweet,
  And honey wild, and manna dew,
And sure in language strange she said,—
    "I love thee true."

'She took me to her elfin grot,
  And there she wept and sighed full sore,
And there I shut her wild wild eyes
    With kisses four.

'And there she lullèd me asleep,
  And there I dreamed—Ah! woe betide!
The latest dream I ever dreamed
    On the cold hill's side.

'I saw pale kings and princes too,
  Pale warriors, death-pale were they all;
They cried—"La belle Dame sans Merci
    Hath thee in thrall!"

'I saw their starved lips in the gloam,
  With horrid warning gapèd wide,
And I awoke and found me here,
    On the cold hill's side.

'And this is why I sojourn here
  Alone and palely loitering,
Though the sedge is withered from the lake,
    And no birds sing.'

from

~ MAUD ~

ALFRED TENNYSON

I have led her home, my love, my only friend.
There is none like her, none.
And never yet so warmly ran my blood
And sweetly, on and on
Calming itself to the long-wished-for end,
Full to the banks, close on the promised good.

None like her, none.
Just now the dry-tongued laurels' pattering talk
Seemed her light foot along the garden walk,
And shook my heart to think she comes once more;
But even then I heard her close the door,
The gates of Heaven are closed, and she is gone.

There is none like her, none.
Nor will be when our summers have deceased.
O, art thou sighing for Lebanon
In the long breeze that streams to thy delicious East,
Sighing for Lebanon,
Dark cedar, tho' thy limbs have here increased,
Upon a pastoral slope as fair,

And looking to the South, and fed
With honeyed rain and delicate air,
And haunted by the starry head
Of her whose gentle will has changed my fate,
And made my life a perfumed altar-flame;
And over whom thy darkness must have spread
With such delights as theirs of old, thy great
Forefathers of the thornless garden, there
Shadowing the snow-limbed Eve from whom she came.

Here will I lie, while these long branches sway,
And you fair stars that crown a happy day
Go in and out as if at merry play,
Who am no more so all forlorn,
As when it seemed far better to be born
To labour and the mattock-hardened hand,
Than nursed at ease and brought to understand
A sad astrology, the boundless plan
That makes you tyrants in your iron skies,
Innumerable, pitiless, passionless eyes,
Cold fires, yet with the power to burn and brand
His nothingness into man.

But now shine on, and what care I,
Who in this stormy gulf have found a pearl
The countercharm of space and hollow sky,
And do accept my madness, and would die
To save from some slight shame one simple girl.

One word is too often profaned
    For me to profane it;
One feeling too falsely disdained
    For thee to disdain it;
One hope is too like despair
    For prudence to smother;
And pity from thee more dear
    Than that from another.

I can give not what men call love:
    But wilt thou accept not
The worship the heart lifts above
    And the heavens reject not,
The desire of the moth for the star,
    Of the night for the morrow,
The devotion to something afar
    From the sphere of our sorrow?

PERCY BYSSHE SHELLEY

~ THE FLIGHT OF LOVE ~

PERCY BYSSHE SHELLEY

When the lamp is shattered
The light in the dust lies dead—
When the cloud is scattered,
The rainbow's glory is shed.
When the lute is broken,
Sweet tones are remembered not;
When the lips have spoken,
Loved accents are soon forgot.

As music and splendour
Survive not the lamp nor the lute,
The heart's echoes render
No song when the spirit is mute—
No song but sad dirges,
Like the wind through a ruined cell,
Or the mournful surges
That ring the dead seaman's knell.

When hearts have once mingled,
Love first leaves the well-built nest;
The weak one is singled
To endure what it once possessed.
O Love! who bewailest
The frailty of all things here,
Why choose you the frailest
For your cradle, your home, and your bier?

Its passions will rock thee
As the storms rock the ravens on high;
Bright reason will mock thee
Like the sun from a wintry sky.
From thy nest every rafter
Will rot, and thine eagle home
Leave thee naked to laughter,
When leaves fall and cold winds come.

~ La Vita Nuova ~

DANTE ALIGHIERI

TRANSLATED BY DANTE GABRIEL ROSSETTI

Mine eyes beheld the blessed pity spring
   Into thy countenance immediately
   A while agone, when thou beheldst in me
The sickness only hidden grief can bring;
And then I knew thou wast considering
   How abject and forlorn my life must be;
   And I became afraid that thou shouldst see
My weeping, and account it a base thing.
Therefore I went out from thee; feeling how
   The tears were straightway loosened at my heart
   Beneath thine eyes' compassionate control;
   And afterwards I said within my soul:
   'Lo! with this lady dwells the counterpart
Of the same Love who holds me weeping now.'

～Dante's Dream～

Dante Gabriel Rossetti

❧

*T*he sun ceased and the stars began to gather,
And each wept at the other;
And birds dropped at midflight out of the sky
And earth shook suddenly:
And I was 'ware of one, hoarse and tired out,
Who asked of me 'Hast thou not heard it said
The lady, she that was so fair, is dead?'
Then lifting up mine eyes, as the tears came,
I saw the angels like a rain of Manna
In a long flight flying back Heavenwards,
Having a little cloud in front of them,
After which they went and said 'Hosanna',
And if they had said more you should have heard.
Then Love spoke thus: 'Now all shall be made clear,
Come and behold our lady where she lies.'
These idle Phantasies
Then carried me to see my lady dead,
And standing at her head
Her ladies put a white veil over her;
And with her was such very humbleness
That she appeared to say 'I am at peace.'

from

～ MARIANA ～

ALFRED TENNYSON

With blackest moss the flower-plots
  Were thickly crusted, one and all:
The rusted nails fell from the knots
  That held the pear to the gable-wall.
The broken sheds look'd sad and strange:
  Unlifted was the clinking latch;
  Weeded and worn the ancient thatch
Upon the lonely moated grange.
    She only said, 'My life is dreary,
      He cometh not,' she said;
    She said, 'I am aweary, aweary,
      I would that I were dead!'

The sparrow's chirrup on the roof,
  The slow clock ticking, and the sound
Which to the wooing wind aloof
  The poplar made, did all confound
Her sense; but most she loathed the hour
  When the thick-moted sunbeam lay
  Athwart the chambers, and the day
Was sloping toward his western bower.
    Then, said she, 'I am very dreary,
      He will not come,' she said;
    She wept, 'I am aweary, aweary,
      Oh God, that I were dead!'

from

~ THE MILLER'S DAUGHTER ~

ALFRED TENNYSON

Love that hath us in the net,
Can we pass, and we forget?
Many suns arise and set.
Many a chance the years beget.
Love the gift is Love the debt.
　　　Even so.
Love is hurt with jar and fret.
Love is made a vague regret.
Eyes with idle tears are wet.
Idle habit links us yet.
What is love? for we forget:
　　　Ah, no! no!

from

~ PRAISE OF MY LADY ~

WILLIAM MORRIS

My lady seems of ivory
Forehead, straight nose, and cheeks that be
Hollowed a little mournfully.
Beata mea Domina!

Her forehead, overshadowed much
By bows of hair, has a wave such
As God was good to make for me.
Beata mea Domina!

Not greatly long my lady's hair,
Nor yet with yellow colour fair,
But thick and crispèd wonderfully:
Beata mea Domina!

Heavy to make the pale face sad,
And dark, but dead as though it had
Been forged by God most wonderfully
—*Beata mea Domina!*—

Of some strange metal, thread by thread,
To stand out from my lady's head,
Not moving much to tangle me.
Beata mea Domina!

Beneath her brows the lids fall slow,
The lashes a clear shadow throw
Where I would wish my lips to be.
Beata mea Domina!

∼ None of ∼
Beauty's Daughters

George Gordon Byron

☙

There be none of Beauty's daughters
    With a magic like Thee;
And like music on the waters
    Is thy sweet voice to me:
When, as if its sound were causing
The charmèd ocean's pausing,
The waves lie still and gleaming,
And the lulled winds seem dreaming:

And the midnight moon is weaving
    Her bright chain o'er the deep,
Whose breast is gently heaving
    As an infant's asleep:
So the spirit bows before thee
To listen and adore thee;
With a full but soft emotion,
Like the swell of Summer's ocean.

~ To ~
One in Paradise

Edgar Allan Poe

🌿

Thou wast all that to me, love,
For which my soul did pine—
A green isle in the sea, love,
A fountain and a shrine,
All wreathed with fairy fruits and flowers,
And all the flowers were mine.

Now all my days are trances,
And all my nightly dreams
Are where thy grey eye glances,
And where thy footstep gleams—
In what ethereal dances,
By what eternal streams!

~ The Blessèd Damozel ~

Dante Gabriel Rossetti

The blessèd damozel leaned out
    From the gold bar of Heaven;
Her eyes were deeper than the depth
    Of waters stilled at even;
She had three lilies in her hand,
    And the stars in her hair were seven.

Her robe, ungirt from clasp to hem,
    No wrought flowers did adorn,
But a white rose of Mary's gift,
    For service meetly worn;
Her hair that lay along her back
    Was yellow like ripe corn.

Herseemed she scarce had been a day
    One of God's choristers;
The wonder was not yet quite gone
    From that still look of hers;
Albeit, to them she left, her day
    Had counted as ten years.

(To one, it is ten years of years.
    . . . Yet now, and in this place,
Surely she leaned o'er me—her hair
    Fell all about my face. . .
Nothing: the autumn-fall of leaves.
    The whole year sets apace.)

THE BLESSED DAMOZEL

It was the rampart of God's house
  That she was standing on;
By God built over the sheer depth
  The which is Space begun;
So high, that looking downward thence
  She scarce could see the sun.

It lies in Heaven, across the flood
  Of ether, as a bridge.
Beneath, the tides of day and night
  With flame and darkness ridge
The void, as low as where this earth
  Spins like a fretful midge.

Around her, lovers, newly met
  'Mid deathless love's acclaims,
Spoke evermore among themselves
  Their heart-remembered names;
And the souls mounting up to God
  Went by her like thin flames.

And still she bowed herself and stooped
  Out of the circling charm;
Until her bosom must have made
  The bar she leaned on warm,
And the lilies lay as if asleep
  Along her bended arm.

From the fixed place of Heaven she saw
    Time like a pulse shake fierce
Through all the worlds. Her gaze still strove
    Within the gulf to pierce
Its path; and now she spoke as when
    The stars sang in their spheres.

The sun was gone now; the curled moon
    Was like a little feather
Fluttering far down the gulf; and now
    She spoke through the still weather.
Her voice was like the voice the stars
    Had when they sang together.

(Ah sweet! Even now, in that bird's song,
    Strove not her accents there,
Fain to be hearkened? When those bells
    Possessed the mid-day air,
Strove not her steps to reach my side
    Down all the echoing stair?)

'I wish that he were come to me,
    For he will come,' she said.
'Have I not prayed in Heaven?—on earth,
    Lord, Lord, has he not prayed?
Are not two prayers a perfect strength?
    And shall I feel afraid?

'When round his head the aureole clings,
    And he is clothed in white,
I'll take his hand and go with him
    To the deep wells of light;
As unto a stream we will step down,
    And bathe there in God's sight.

'We two will stand beside that shrine,
    Occult, withheld, untrod,
Whose lamps are stirred continually
    With prayer sent up to God;
And see our old prayers, granted, melt
    Each like a little cloud.

'We two will lie i' the shadow of
    That living mystic tree
Within whose secret growth the Dove
    Is sometimes felt to be,
While every leaf that His plumes touch
    Saith His Name audibly.

'And I myself will teach to him,
    I myself, lying so,
The songs I sing here; which his voice
    Shall pause in, hushed and slow,
And find some knowledge at each pause,
    Or some new thing to know.'

(Alas! we two, we two, thou say'st!
    Yea, one wast thou with me
That once of old. But shall God lift
    To endless unity
The soul whose likeness with thy soul
    Was but its love for thee?)

'We two,' she said, 'will seek the groves
    Where the lady Mary is,
With her five handmaidens, whose names
    Are five sweet symphonies,
Cecily, Gertrude, Magdalen,
    Margaret and Rosalys.

'Circlewise sit they, with bound locks
    And foreheads garlanded;
Into the fine cloth white like flame
    Weaving the golden thread,
To fashion the birth-robes for them
    Who are just born, being dead.

'He shall fear, haply, and be dumb:
    Then will I lay my cheek
To his, and tell about our love,
    Not once abashed or weak:
And the dear Mother will approve
    My pride, and let me speak.

'Herself shall bring us, hand in hand,
    To Him round whom all souls
Kneel, the clear-ranged unnumbered heads
    Bowed with their aureoles:
And angels meeting us shall sing
    To their citherns and citoles.

'There will I ask of Christ the Lord
    Thus much for him and me: —
Only to live as once on earth
    With Love, — only to be,
As then awhile, for ever now
    Together, I and he.'

She gazed and listened and then said,
　　Less sad of speech than mild, —
'All this is when he comes.' She ceased.
　　The light thrilled towards her, fill'd
With angels in strong level flight.
　　Her eyes prayed, and she smil'd.

(I saw her smile.) But soon their path
　　Was vague in distant spheres:
And then she cast her arms along
　　The golden barriers,
And laid her face between her hands,
　　And wept. (I heard her tears.)

～ *R*EST ～

CHRISTINA ROSSETTI

O Earth, lie heavily upon her eyes;
   Seal her sweet eyes weary of watching, Earth;
   Lie close around her; leave no room for mirth
With its harsh laughter, nor for sound of sighs.
She hath no questions, she hath no replies,
   Hushed in and curtained with a blessèd dearth
   Of all that irked her from the hour of birth;
With stillness that is almost Paradise.
Darkness more clear than noonday holdeth her,
   Silence more musical than any song;
Even her very heart has ceased to stir:
Until the morning of Eternity
Her rest shall not begin nor end, but be;
   And when she wakes she will not think it long.

∼ Venus Verticordia ∼

DANTE GABRIEL ROSSETTI

❧

She hath the apple in her hand for thee,
   Yet almost in her heart would hold it back;
   She muses, with her eyes upon the track
Of that which in thy spirit they can see.
Haply, 'Behold, he is at peace,' saith she;
   'Alas! the apple for his lips, — the dart
   That follows its brief sweetness to his heart, —
The wandering of his feet perpetually!'

A little space her glance is still and coy;
   But if she give the fruit that works her spell,
Those eyes shall flame as for her Phrygian boy.
   Then shall her bird's strained throat the woe foretell,
   And her far seas moan as a single shell,
And through her dark grove strike the light of Troy.

~A Birthday~

Christina Rossetti

My heart is like a singing bird
    Whose nest is in a watered shoot;
My heart is like an apple tree
    Whose boughs are bent with thick-set fruit;
My heart is like a rainbow shell
    That paddles in a halcyon sea;
My heart is gladder than all these
    Because my love is come to me.

Raise me a dais of silk and down;
    Hang it with vair and purple dyes;
Carve it in doves and pomegranates,
    And peacocks with a hundred eyes;
Work it in gold and silver grapes,
    In leaves and silver fleurs-de-lys;
Because the birthday of my life
    Is come, my love is come to me.

~ TIME OF ROSES ~

THOMAS HOOD

It was not in the Winter
    Our loving lot was cast;
It was the time of roses—
    We plucked them as we passed!

That churlish season never frowned
    On early lovers yet:
O no—the world was newly crowned
    With flowers when first we met!

'Twas twilight, and I bade you go,
    But still you held me fast;
It was the time of roses—
    We plucked them as we passed!

~ PROSERPINE ~

DANTE GABRIEL ROSSETTI

Afar away the light that brings cold cheer
   Unto this wall,—one instant and no more
   Admitted at my distant palace-door.
Afar the flowers of Enna from this drear
Dire fruit, which, tasted once, must thrall me here.
   Afar those skies from this Tartarean grey
   That chills me: and afar, how far away,
The nights that shall be from the days that were.

Afar from mine own self I seem, and wing
   Strange ways in thought, and listen for a sign:
   And still some heart unto some soul doth pine,
(Whose sounds mine inner sense is fain to bring,
Continually together murmuring)—
   "Woe's me for thee, unhappy Proserpine!"

∼ THE STORY OF ∼
CUPID AND PSYCHE

WILLIAM MORRIS

Within the flicker of a white-thorn shade
In gentle sleep he found the maiden laid.
One hand that held a book had fallen away
Across her body, and the other lay
Upon a marble fountain's plashing rim,
Among whose broken waves the fish showed dim,
But yet its wide-flung spray now woke her not,
Because the summer day at noon was hot,
And all sweet sounds and scents were lulling her.

   So soon the rustle of his wings 'gan stir
Her looser folds of raiment, and the hair
Spread wide upon the grass and daisies fair,
As Love cast down his eyes with a half smile
Godlike and cruel; that faded in a while,
And long he stood above her hidden eyes
With red lips parted in a god's surprise.

   Then very Love knelt down beside the maid
And on her breast a hand unfelt he laid,
And drew the gown from off her dainty feet,
And set his fair cheek to her shoulder sweet,
And kissed her lips that knew of no love yet,
And wondered if his heart would e'er forget
The perfect arm that o'er her body lay.

THE NYMPH'S SONG
~TO HYLAS~

WILLIAM MORRIS

I know a little garden-close
Set thick with lily and red rose,
Where I would wander if I might
From dewy dawn to dewy night,
And have one with me wandering.

And though within it no birds sing,
And though no pillared house is there,
And though the apple boughs are bare
Of fruit and blossom, would to God,
Her feet upon the green grass trod,
And I beheld them as before!

There comes a murmur from the shore,
And in the place two fair streams are,
Drawn from the purple hills afar,
Drawn down unto the restless sea;
The hills whose flowers ne'er fed the bee,
The shore no ship has ever seen,
Still beaten by the billows green,
Whose murmur comes unceasingly
Unto the place for which I cry.

For which I cry both day and night,
For which I let slip all delight,
That maketh me both deaf and blind,
Careless to win, unskilled to find,
And quick to lose what all men seek.

Yet tottering as I am, and weak,
Still have I left a little breath
To seek within the jaws of death
An entrance to that happy place;
To seek the unforgotten face
Once seen, once kissed, once reft from me
Anigh the murmuring of the sea.

from

~ *A* MATCH ~

ALGERNON CHARLES SWINBURNE

If love were what the rose is,
　And I were like the leaf,
Our lives would grow together
In sad or singing weather,
Blown fields or flowerful closes,
　Green pleasure or grey grief;
If love were what the rose is,
　And I were like the leaf.

If I were what the words are,
　And love were like the tune,
With double sound and single
Delight our lips would mingle,
With kisses glad as birds are
　That get sweet rain at noon;
If I were what the words are,
　And love were like the tune.

If you were life, my darling,
　And I your love were death,
We'd shine and snow together
Ere March made sweet the weather
With daffodil and starling
　And hours of fruitful breath;
If you were life, my darling,
　And I your love were death.

If you were April's lady,
    And I were lord in May,
We'd throw with leaves for hours
And draw for days with flowers,
Till day like night were shady,
    And night were bright like day;
If you were April's lady,
    And I were lord in May.

If you were queen of pleasure,
  And I were king of pain,
We'd hunt down love together,
Pluck out his flying feather,
And teach his feet a measure,
  And find his mouth a rein;
If you were queen of pleasure,
  And I were king of pain.

~ THE BEGGAR MAID ~

ALFRED TENNYSON

Her arms across her breast she laid;
 She was more fair than words can say:
Bare-footed came the beggar maid
 Before the king Cophetua.
In robe and crown the king stept down,
 To meet and greet her on her way;
'It is no wonder,' said the lords,
 'She is more beautiful than day.'

As shines the moon in clouded skies,
 She in her poor attire was seen:
One praised her ankles, one her eyes,
 One her dark hair and lovesome mien.
So sweet a face, such angel grace,
 In all that land had never been:
Cophetua swore a royal oath:
 'This beggar maid shall be my queen!'

～ Evening ～

John Clare

'Tis evening, the black snail has got on his track,
And gone to its nest is the wren;—
And the packman snail too, with his home on his back;
Clings on the bowed bents like a wen.

The shepherd has made a rude mark with his foot,
Where his shadow reached when he first came;
And it just touched the tree where his secret love cut,
Two letters that stand for love's name.

The evening comes in with the wishes of love; —
And the shepherd he looks on the flowers; —
And thinks who would praise the soft song of the dove,
And meet joy in these dewfalling hours.

For nature is love, and the wishers of love;
When nothing can hear or intrude;
It hides from the eagle, and joins with the dove:
In beautiful green solitude.

∽ GIVE ALL TO LOVE ∽

RALPH WALDO EMERSON

Give all to love;
Obey thy heart;
Friends, kindred, days,
Estate, good fame,
Plans, credit, and the Muse—
Nothing refuse.

'Tis a brave master;
Let it have scope:
Follow it utterly,
Hope beyond hope:
High and more high
It dives into noon,
With wing unspent,
Untold intent;
But it is a god,
Knows its own path,
And the outlets of the sky.

It was never for the mean;
It requireth courage stout,
Souls above doubt,
Valour unbending:
Such 'twill reward;—
They shall return
More than they were,
And ever ascending.

Leave all for love;
Yet, hear me, yet,
One more word thy heart behoved,
One pulse more of firm endeavour—
Keep thee today,
Tomorrow, for ever,
Free as an Arab
Of thy beloved.

Cling with life to the maid;
But when the surprise,
First vague shadow of surmise,
Flits across her bosom young,
Of a joy apart from thee,
Free be she, fancy-free;
Nor thou detain her vesture's hem,
Nor the palest rose she flung
From her summer diadem.

Thou thou loved her as thyself,
As a self of purer clay;
Though her parting dims the day,
Stealing grace from all alive;
Heartily know,
When half-gods go
The gods arrive.

~ ℱINIS ~

WALTER SAVAGE LANDOR

I strove with none, for none was worth my strife:
   Nature I loved, and, next to Nature, Art:
I warmed both hands before the fire of Life;
   It sinks; and I am ready to depart.

~ INDEX OF ARTISTS AND PAINTINGS ~

(The dates of the paintings are given where known)

FRONT & BACK COVER AND PAGES 20-21 *above*
Love among the Ruins (1894) *detail*
Sir Edward Burne-Jones (1833-1898)
The National Trust, Wightwick Manor

PAGE 5 *above*
Pygmalion and the Image IV:
The Soul Attains (1868-78)
Sir Edward Burne-Jones
Birmingham Museums & Art Gallery

PAGE 9 *left*
Sancta Lilas (1874) *detail*
Dante Gabriel Rossetti
(1828-1882)
Tate Gallery, London

PAGE 10 *right*
The March Marigold
(c.1870) *detail*
Sir Edward Burne-Jones
*Piccadilly Gallery,
London*

PAGE 13 *left*
The Golden Stairs (1880) *detail*
Sir Edward Burne-Jones
Tate Gallery, London

PAGES 14-15 *above*
The Rose Bower from the Briar Rose
series (1870-90) *detail*
Sir Edward Burne-Jones
*Faringdon Collection Trust,
Buscot Park*

PAGE 16 *above*
The Briar Wood (1869)
detail
Sir Edward Burne-Jones
The Maas Gallery, London

PAGE 19 *right*
Danaë or The Tower of Brass (1887-88)
Sir Edward Burne-Jones
*Glasgow Museums: Art Gallery
and Museum, Kelvingrove*

PAGE 23 *left*
Lady Lilith (1864-68)
Dante Gabriel Rossetti
*Delaware Art Museum
(Samuel and Mary R. Bancroft
Memorial, 1935)*

PAGE 24 *right*
Elizabeth Siddal (1855)
Dante Gabriel Rossetti
Ashmolean Museum, Oxford

PAGE 27 *above*
The Beguiling of Merlin (1870-74)
detail
Sir Edward Burne-Jones
*Lady Lever Art Gallery, Port Sunlight
Board of Trustees: National Museums
& Galleries on Merseyside*

PAGE 28 *above*
La Belle Dame sans Merci
(1893) *detail*
John William Waterhouse
(1849-1917)
*Hessisches Landesmuseum,
Darmstadt*

PAGE 33 *above*
Sponsa de Libano (1891)
Sir Edward Burne-Jones
*Walker Art Gallery, Liverpool
Board of Trustees:
National Museums & Galleries
on Merseyside*

PAGES 34-35 and endpapers *above*
Laus Veneris (1873-75) *detail*
Sir Edward Burne-Jones
Laing Art Gallery,
Newcastle-upon-Tyne

PAGE 37 *above*
A Christmas Carol (1867)
Dante Gabriel Rossetti
Private Collection

PAGE 39 *above*
Donna della Finestra *detail*
Dante Gabriel Rossetti
Birmingham Museums
& Art Gallery

PAGE 40 *above*
Dante's Dream (1856) *detail*
Dante Gabriel Rossetti
Tate Gallery, London

PAGE 43 *left*
Mariana in the Moated Grange
(1851) *detail*
Sir John Everett Millais
(1829-1896)
The Makins Collection

PAGE 44 *right*
April Love (1855-56)
Arthur Hughes (1832-1915)
Tate Gallery, London

PAGE 47 *above*
La Belle Iseult
William Morris (1834-1896)
Tate Gallery, London

PAGE 49 *above*
The Mirror of Venus (1898)
detail
Sir Edward Burne-Jones
*Museu Calouste Gulbenkian,
Lisbon*

PAGE 50 *above*
In the Grass
Arthur Hughes
Sheffield City Art Galleries

PAGES 53 and 59 (*detail*) *above*
The Blessèd Damozel (1875-78)
Dante Gabriel Rossetti
*Fogg Art Museum,
Harvard University Art Museums,
Bequest of Grenville L. Winthrop*

PAGE 57 *left*
Study for the Blessèd Damozel
(1876)
Dante Gabriel Rossetti
Manchester City Art Galleries

PAGE 60 *right*
Beata Beatrix (1864-70) *detail*
Dante Gabriel Rossetti
Tate Gallery, London

PAGE 63 *left*
Venus Verticordia (1864-68)
Dante Gabriel Rossetti
*Russell-Cotes Art Gallery
and Museum, Bournemouth*

PAGE 64 *above*
Pomona
Sir Edward Burne-Jones,
(tapestry made by
Morris & Co. c.1885)
*Harris Museum and
Art Gallery, Preston,
Lancashire*

PAGE 67 *above*
Early Lovers (1858)
Frederick Smallfield (1829-1915)
Manchester City Art Galleries

PAGE 69 *left*
Proserpine (1874)
Dante Gabriel Rossetti
Tate Gallery, London

PAGE 70 *above*
Cupid Finding Psyche Asleep
by a Fountain *detail*
Sir Edward Burne-Jones
Birmingham Museums & Art Gallery

PAGE 72 *above*
Hylas and the Nymphs (1896) *detail*
John William Waterhouse
Manchester City Art Galleries

PAGE 74 *above*
A Study for a Naiad
John William Waterhouse
Bonhams, London

PAGES 76-77 *above*
The Love Song
Sir Edward Burne-Jones
The Metropolitan Museum of Art, New York
The Alfred N. Punnett Endowment Fund, 1947 (47.26)

PAGES 80-81 *above*
Green Summer (1868) *detail*
Sir Edward Burne-Jones
Christie's Images

PAGE 85 *below*
Mrs William Morris (1873)
Dante Gabriel Rossetti
Private Collection

PAGE 78 *above*
King Cophetua and the Beggar
Maid (1884)
Sir Edward Burne-Jones
Tate Gallery, London

PAGE 82 *right*
The Temple of Love
Sir Edward Burne-Jones
Tate Gallery, London

~Index of Poetry~

PHOTOGRAPHIC ACKNOWLEDGEMENTS

For permission to reproduce the paintings on the following pages and for
supplying photographs, the Publishers would like to thank:

Birmingham Museums & Art Gallery: 5, 39, 70
Bridgeman Art Library: 10, 16, 24, 27, 28, 33, 34-35, 43, 49, 50, 63,
64, 67, 72, 74, 80-81, endpapers
Delaware Art Museum: 23
Faringdon Collection Trust: 14-15
Courtesy of the Fogg Art Museum, Harvard University Art Museums: 53, 59
Glasgow Museums: Art Gallery and Museum, Kelvingrove: 19
© Manchester City Art Galleries: 57
The Metropolitan Museum of Art: 76-77
National Trust Photographic Library/Derrick E. Witty: front & back cover, 20-21
Sotheby's Picture Library: 37, 85
© Tate Gallery, London: 9, 13, 40, 44, 47, 60, 69, 78, 82